Famous Women in History

NELLIE BLY
INTREPID REPORTER

AMIE JANE LEAVITT

Paperback ISBN 979-8-89094-146-6
Hardcover ISBN 979-8-89094-147-3

Library of Congress Control Number: 2024946983

To learn more about the other great books from Fox Chapel Publishing, or to find a retailer near you, call toll-free 800-457-9112, send mail to , 903 Square Street, Mount Joy, PA 17552, or visit us at ***www.FoxChapelPublishing.com.***

We are always looking for talented authors. To submit an idea, please send a brief inquiry to acquisitions@foxchapelpublishing.com.

Fox Chapel Publishing makes every effort to use environmentally friendly paper for printing.

Printed in China

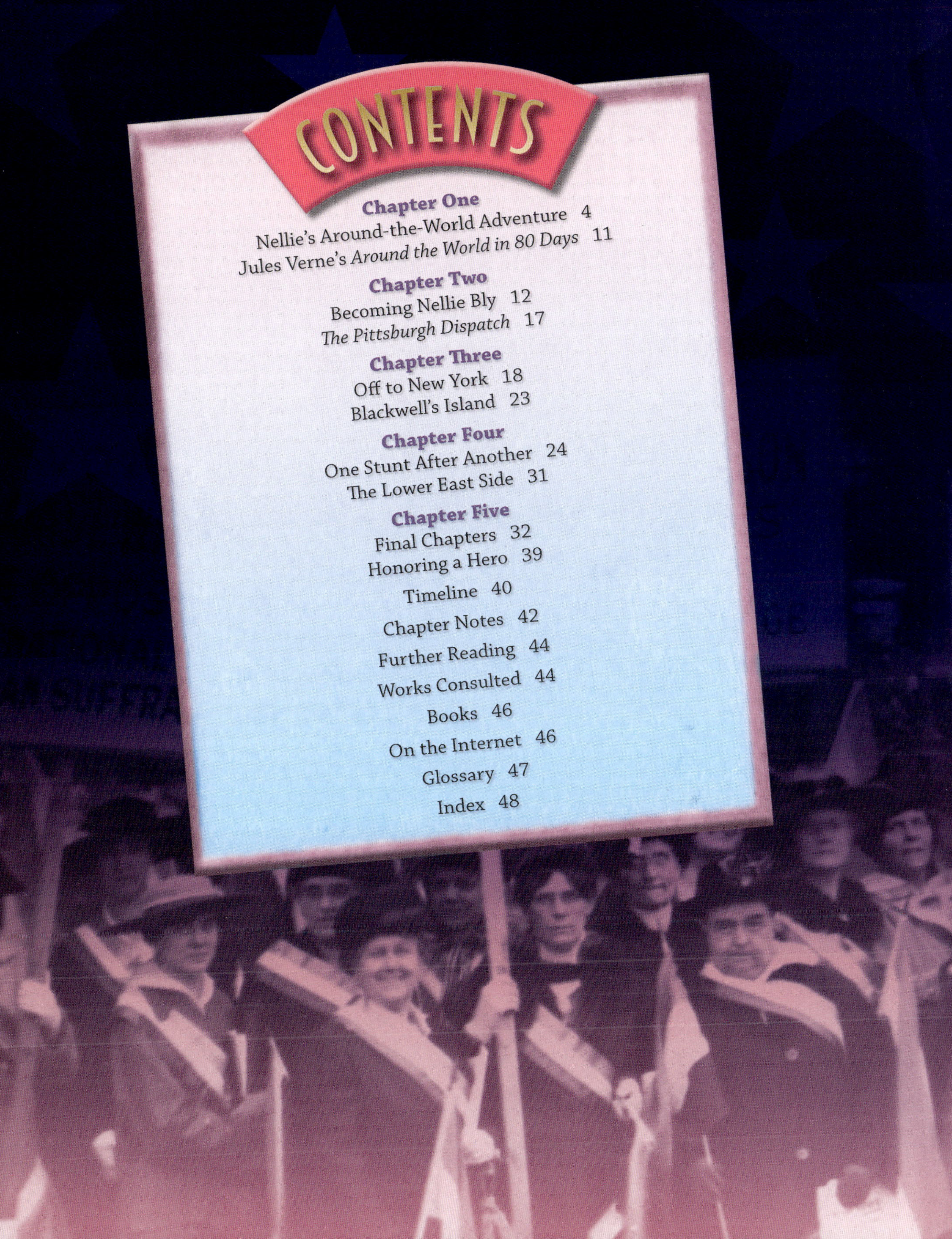

CONTENTS

Chapter One
Nellie's Around-the-World Adventure 4
Jules Verne's *Around the World in 80 Days* 11

Chapter Two
Becoming Nellie Bly 12
The Pittsburgh Dispatch 17

Chapter Three
Off to New York 18
Blackwell's Island 23

Chapter Four
One Stunt After Another 24
The Lower East Side 31

Chapter Five
Final Chapters 32
Honoring a Hero 39

Timeline 40

Chapter Notes 42

Further Reading 44

Works Consulted 44

Books 46

On the Internet 46

Glossary 47

Index 48

CHAPTER ONE

On November 14, 1889, Nellie Bly boarded the *Augusta Victoria* in New Jersey. The sky was clear and sunny, and the bay was calm. It was the perfect day to embark on a journey around the world.[1]

It took seven days to cross the Atlantic Ocean from New Jersey to London. At first, Nellie got quite seasick. She had never been on a ship before, so it took her a while to get used to it. Once she did, though, she never got sick again for the entire trip.[2]

Nellie arrived in London on November 21. She toured the city for a day, then dashed off to France to meet the author, Jules Verne. His book *Around the World in 80 Days* had inspired her trip. He and his wife showed Nellie a map on their wall that compared her travel route with the route of his book character Phileas Fogg. Verne said, "If you do it in 79 days, I shall applaud you with both hands."[3]

The first regular steamship crossings between North America and Europe began in the late 1840s. By the time Jules Verne (top) wrote *Around the World in 80 Days*, travel by steamship was very popular. His character, Phileas Fogg, begins his journey via steamship. Nellie Bly did, too.

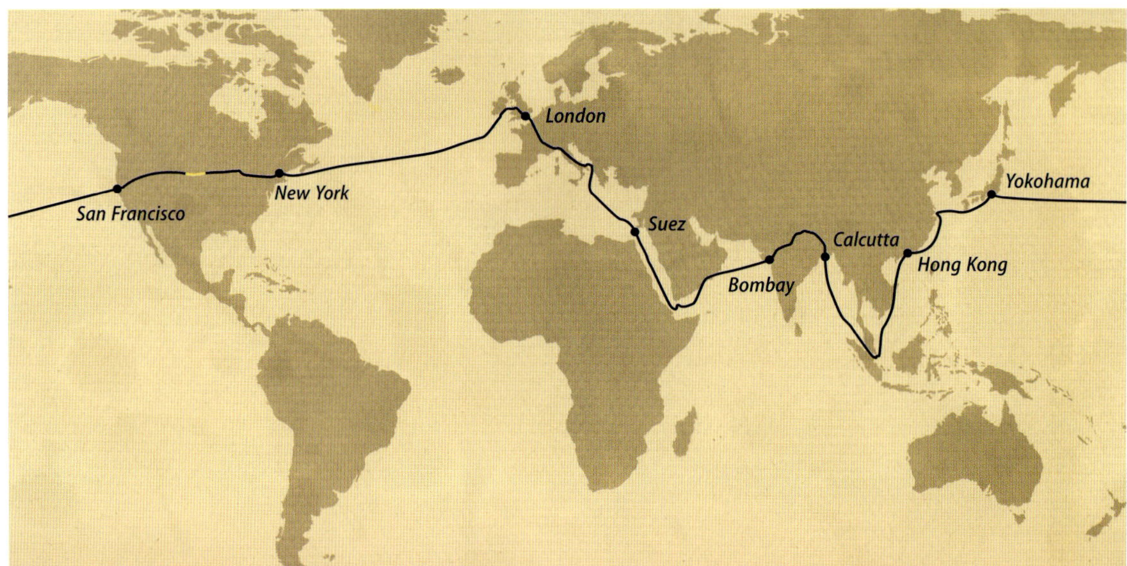

The route of Phileas Fogg. Fogg started his journey in London and then headed east. Many people have tried to recreate his journey, but Nellie Bly was the first to achieve it.

From France, Nellie traveled to Italy on a train. It was cold and foggy most of the time, so she only got to see a little of the country as they moved along the tracks. There was no time for sightseeing. At the station, she immediately boarded a ship to sale across the Mediterranean.

The ship arrived in Port Said, Egypt, on November 27. At this port, the ship's passengers walked across a sandy beach and into town. Nellie saw many things she wanted to buy but had decided to pack light on her travels. She only brought one small handbag and no other luggage, so she didn't have room for souvenirs.[4] However, Nellie purchased one item—a sunhat that she could carry on her head. Later, as passengers made their way back to the ship, Nellie spotted a camel train arriving at the train station from the desert.[5]

After crossing through the Suez Canal, they sailed south on the Red Sea for five days. The weather turned hot, which made Nellie appreciate her new sunhat. At night, many passengers slept on the deck chairs to stay cool in the sea breeze. During the day, passengers entertained themselves by putting on shows like singing, dancing, and performing comedy.[6]

They docked for a day in Aden, Yemen. The captain thought it best that all passengers stay aboard since it was so hot. But Nellie came to see the world, not just the inside of a ship. She went into town for the day with a few other passengers. They rode a carriage through the smooth, wide streets, saw the small adobe houses in town, and watched the blue-silver water lapping in the bay.

They then sailed across the Indian Ocean for Sri Lanka. The island was beautiful, with its feathery palms and green mountains surrounded by a blue sea. Nellie and the other passengers stayed in a hotel for five days in the port of Columbo. She hadn't planned to stay that long, but the ship was delayed in leaving. Making the best of it, Nellie tried curry for the first time, drove in a car to the top of a mountain, rode through town in a rickshaw, and went to the theater.[7]

The next stop was Penang in Malaysia. In the few hours she

A rickshaw in 1900. Rickshaws are still used in some countries, but outlawed in others due to concerns with rickshaw driver safety.

Sampans are Chinese flat-bottomed wooden boats.

was there, Nellie rode in a flat-bottomed boat called a sampan, saw a waterfall and tropical garden, and visited a Hindu temple. The next day, the ship docked in Singapore for 24 hours. Passengers toured the port just as they had at other stops, but this day was different. Nellie decided to buy another souvenir, but it was nothing she could store in her handbag or wear on her head. She bought a pet monkey! She wanted it to be her companion on her journey back home to America.

Nellie tried to send telegrams back to her newspaper editor in New York as often as she could. There weren't telegraph offices in every port, so it was difficult to get word to the editor. Sometimes, she just sent notes back by mail, but it often took too long to get there. There were many people following Nellie's adventure by reading stories about her in the newspaper. Readers started a game where they would guess how long it took her to get home. Nellie appreciated the support and overwhelming interest in her travels. She knew

Telegraphs were the text-messaging technology of the 1800s.

it would draw attention to her articles once she got home.

In Hong Kong, China, she found out that another newspaper had sent a reporter out to do the same thing she was doing. Elizabeth Bisland left New York just six hours after Nellie did. But instead of going east, Elizabeth went west. Nellie didn't pay much mind to someone "racing" her. She was determined to beat Phileas Fogg's 80-day record, aiming to travel around the world in 75 days. If someone else wanted to do it faster, that wasn't Nellie's concern. But time was slipping away! If Nellie wanted to get home in time, she had to get moving! She couldn't allow any more delays.[8]

Phileas Fogg purchases an elephant to continue on his journey in this illustration from *Around the World in 80 Days*.

Nellie left Yokohama, Japan on January 7 on the steamship *Oceanic*. It took two weeks to cross the massive Pacific Ocean. She finally arrived in San Francisco on January 21. Crowds of people greeted Nellie at the dock. Her newspaper arranged for a special train to take her across the country. They traveled quickly, only making a few stops on the way.

Nellie Bly arrives in New Jersey on January 25, 1890. She had made it all the way around the world in 72 days.

Nellie's favorite stop was Pittsburgh, the town where she started as a reporter. Many of her friends were there to cheer her on!

Nellie arrived in New Jersey on January 25. Thousands of people packed into the station awaiting her arrival. When she stepped down onto the platform, crowds cheered and cannons boomed. She made it! Nellie beat Phileas Fogg's record as well as the other female reporter. Better yet, she beat her own goal. She traveled around the world in 72 days, 6 hours, and 11 minutes.[9]

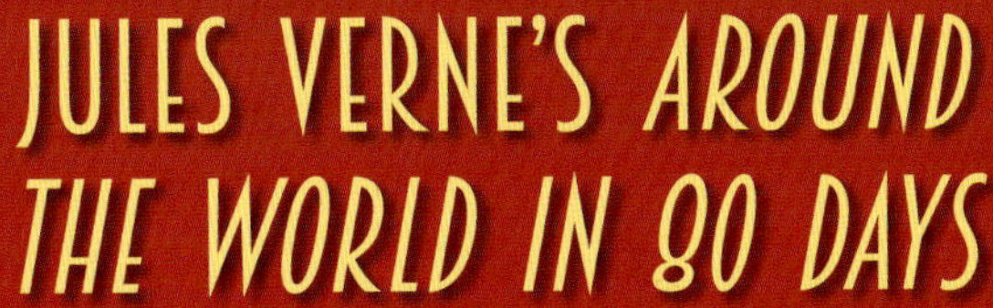

Jules Verne's *Around the World in 80 Days*

Jules Verne was a famous author in the 1800s. His book *Around the World in 80 Days* was published in 1872. This book follows the fictional character Phileas Fogg as he travels around the world.

Verne came up with the idea by reading a scientific article in a newspaper. The article used math calculations to show that it might be possible to get all the way around the world in 80 days. Verne was intrigued by that idea and used it as the starting point for his book.

Nellie Bly's path was almost the same as Phileas Fogg's path. Nellie stopped at many of the same places, too, and took similar modes of transportation. The main difference in their journey: Fogg started in London and Nellie started in New York.

Around the World in 80 Days has inspired many other travelers. In 2017, Mark Beaumont from Great Britain decided to follow Fogg's journey—except he decided to do it by cycling across the land routes and flying over the ocean. He completed his journey in 78 days, 14 hours, and 40 minutes.

An early copy of *Around the World in 80 Days*

Nellie Bly was one of the most famous female journalists of her time. She was popular long before she went on her trip around the world. But this trip pushed her into greater stardom. As a man in Europe would tell her in 1914, "Every child seven years old in America knows Nellie Bly!"[1]

Nellie Bly wasn't always Nellie Bly. She was born Elizabeth Jane Cochran. She sometimes spelled it "Cochrane." She began using the pen name of Nellie Bly when she started as a newspaper journalist. Many writers, especially female writers, wrote with pen names during that time period. Nellie chose her name based on a popular song by Stephen Foster.[2]

Elizabeth Jane Cochran was born on May 5, 1864, in Cochran's Mills, Pennsylvania. She was one of the youngest children of a very large family. Her father had been married previously and had 10 children with his first wife. He and his second wife, Mary Jane,

Nellie had this suit dress made specially for her trip around the world. Her small handbag is the only luggage she took on the trip.

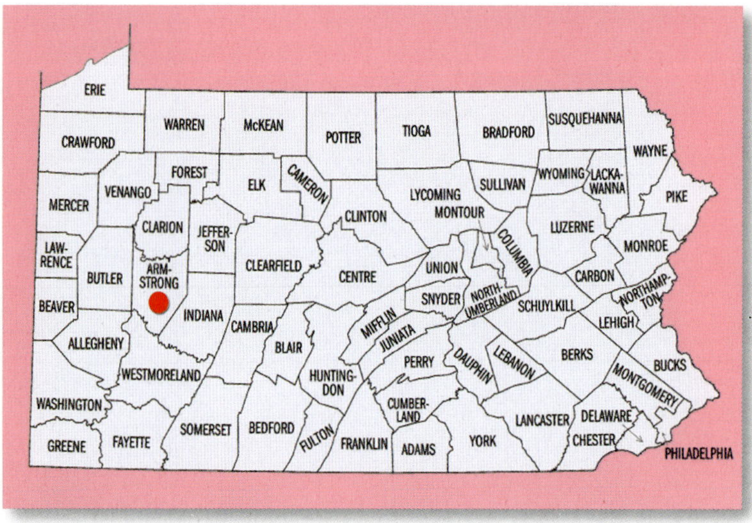

Cochrans Mills (red dot) is in Armstrong County, Pennsylvania.

had five children together. When Elizabeth was little, her mother often dressed her in pink. Most children were dressed in grays or other plain colors, so this made Elizabeth stand out. People began calling her "Pink."

Michael Cochran, Elizabeth's father, was a very successful business owner and judge. The town where Elizabeth was born was named after him. When Elizabeth was only six years old, he died suddenly and didn't have a will. Elizabeth, some of her other siblings, and their mother were left unable to maintain their land and home.

Mary Jane soon remarried. Her new husband was cruel and abusive. Mary Jane finally sued him for divorce. Elizabeth had to be a witness at the divorce hearing against her stepfather.

Elizabeth had been schooled mainly at home. When she was 15, she enrolled at the State Normal School in Indiana, Pennsylvania (now known as Indiana University of Pennsylvania). She hoped to become a teacher so that she could support herself and her mother. But they just didn't have the money for her to continue going. She had to drop out after one semester.[3]

Unmarried women with no inheritance found life to be very difficult in the 1800s. It's not like today, when women can go out and get an education and good jobs. Back then, very few opportunities were available to women. They could work as nurses or teachers, run boardinghouses, or work in factories, but other choices were discouraged.

When it didn't work out for Elizabeth to become a teacher, she and her mother ran a boardinghouse in Pittsburgh, Pennsylvania. During this time, Elizabeth read a story in the paper that criticized women, especially working women. Elizabeth was furious. She wrote a letter to the editor expressing her outrage. She described the plight of women, the difficult lives they often had to lead, and the limited opportunities that were available to them. The editor was so impressed by Elizabeth's letter that he gave her a job as a reporter. When she started working for *The Pittsburgh Dispatch*, she began using the pen name of Nellie Bly.[4]

Nellie wanted to be a serious journalist who wrote important articles about real problems that people faced in the community. She tackled topics that people didn't usually talk about. She wrote about the working conditions in factories. She wrote about what it was like to live in the slums, or poor areas of town. To get the material for her stories, she went to these

Nellie Bly wrote with pluck and courage, and readers looked forward to her stories.

places and interviewed the people who worked and lived there. Once she even pretended she was a factory worker and spent a day working at the job herself to see what it was really like.

Nellie's pieces were very popular with readers, but the local business owners were not so happy that she was making their businesses look bad. They threatened to stop advertising in the paper. As a result, Nellie's editors assigned her articles that were more "appropriate" for female writers and would be less controversial. She was asked to write articles on such topics as fashion, home decorating, gardening, and society. Nellie did not enjoy writing these types of articles. In fact, they bored her. She was itching to do something more important.[5]

Nellie was tired of writing fluff articles for the paper. In 1885, at only 21 years old, she quit the paper and began working as a freelance journalist. As a foreign correspondent, she moved to Mexico and wrote stories about the problems she saw there. She wrote about poverty and about government corruption. When she sent her stories back to the *Dispatch*, they readily agreed to pay her for the right to publish them.

After just six months in Mexico, though, Nellie had to flee the country. The government was not happy about the truth that she was exposing. They wanted to arrest her. Later, she wrote a book about her adventures called *Six Months in Mexico*.[6]

Bly's *Six Months in Mexico* was published in 1888.

THE PITTSBURGH DISPATCH

During Nellie Bly's lifetime, *The Pittsburgh Dispatch* was a popular national newspaper in the United States. It didn't just publish local articles about Western Pennsylvania. It also published articles about events happening around the United States and the world.

Many papers at that time used national and international stories from the Associated Press. The stories were mostly the same in all the papers. *The Pittsburgh Dispatch* didn't do that. It hired its own correspondents and sent them to various places around the globe. It wasn't that unusual, then, that *The Pittsburgh Dispatch* agreed to publish the freelance stories of Nellie Bly while she was in Mexico.

The Pittsburgh Dispatch published its first article on February 9, 1846. The paper was four pages long and cost one penny. The paper's first owner, Colonel J. Heron Foster, was a forward-thinking businessman. He didn't agree with slavery. He also believed in women's rights. He put his beliefs into action when he hired a woman to work in the newsroom.

The last paper at *The Pittsburgh Dispatch* was published on Valentine's Day, February 14, 1923.

CHAPTER THREE

When Nellie returned from Mexico, *The Pittsburgh Dispatch* offered her a job as an arts reporter. She wasn't too thrilled about the position, but decided to give it a try. She wanted to do more serious writing instead of things that the editors thought were appropriate for female writers. After three months, she had enough. She left a note for her editor and didn't show up for work the next morning. The note read: "I am off for New York. Look out for me. Bly."[1]

New York was brimming with excitement in 1887, and Nellie Bly was naturally drawn to it. As soon as she arrived, she started looking for work. She went to newspaper after newspaper but received the same chilly response: No. They did not want to hire a female reporter.

Finally, she went to the *New York World*, owned by Joseph Pulitzer. The managing editor, John Cockerill, hired her on the condition that she prove herself.

During Bly's lifetime, not much was known about mental illness. Psychiatry was a fairly new science. At that time, women could be committed to asylums by their husbands. They didn't even have to have a medical examination. Many of these women started showing the signs of mental illness because of the horrible conditions and treatment they received at the asylum. Once committed, it was nearly impossible to get out on one's own.

New York City Asylum for the Insane. Mental hospitals in the 1800s did not give the same quality of medical care and treatment that institutions do today.

She would have to go undercover on a dangerous and daring assignment. She had to pretend she was mentally ill and get committed to the city's insane asylum for women. Then, after witnessing firsthand the conditions there, she would write an article for the *New York World*.

Nellie was nervous at first, worried that she may not be able to get out of the asylum once she got in. The editor promised that if she got into trouble, the paper would get her released. She shook hands and agreed to do it.[2]

For the assignment, Nellie took on another fake name: Nellie Brown. She pretended to have an accent and know very little English. She checked into a boardinghouse in New York. Then, she started practicing her act.

At first, Nellie thought it would be close to impossible to get committed to the asylum. After all, she would have to convince doctors that she belonged there. And surely, she thought, they would be able to tell she was faking it. Nellie soon realized she was wrong. At that time, it seemed that just about anyone could be forced into an asylum, even if they didn't belong there.

All Nellie did was start acting a little nervous, distracted, and stressed at the

Nellie practiced her fits of insanity in a mirror.

boardinghouse. The woman who ran the house didn't like this behavior, so she called the authorities. She then was taken before a judge, who called a doctor because he thought she was acting strange due to being drugged. The judge felt sympathy for Nellie, saying, "She looks like my sister, and anyone can see she is a good girl." When the doctor surveyed her, he concluded she was taking drugs, so he decided to have her taken to the hospital.[3] She was first taken to Bellevue, a hospital in the city, where she convinced more doctors of her insanity. She was then transferred to the insane asylum on Blackwell's Island.

A judge, with guidance from a doctor, ordered Nellie to the asylum.

Once Nellie got to Blackwell's Island, she stopped her act. "I made no attempt to keep up the assumed role of insanity," she explained. "I talked and acted just as I do in ordinary life. Yet strange to say, the more sanely I talked and acted the crazier I was thought to be."[4]

The conditions at the asylum were much worse than Nellie could have ever imagined. The women were given badly prepared or even rotten food and some were threatened with punishment if they didn't eat it. They were forced to take ice cold baths and sleep in freezing cold rooms. When Nellie asked why there weren't warmer clothing or blankets, the nurses said that Nellie shouldn't "expect any kindness here, for you won't get it."[5]

Inmates were rarely allowed to walk around outside.

Nellie spent ten days inside New York's Blackwell's Island asylum for women. She was horrified by what she saw there and what she personally experienced. She was also shocked by how easily the doctors committed her. She believed that many of the other women didn't belong in the asylum any more than she did. Nellie had found from her own experience that all someone had to do was say a person was acting strange and that would be enough to get them committed to an asylum. Once committed, many patients could not leave. They had to spend the rest of their lives behind these locked doors.

When Nellie had enough material for her story, she told the doctors that she had made it all up, that she wasn't insane. They didn't believe her. However, one considerate doctor moved her to a quieter ward with less cruel conditions. Finally, a lawyer arrived, granting Nellie the option to leave. She quickly consented, but she couldn't help but feel awful about leaving the others behind; so many of them sane.

Bly detailed her experiences in a series of articles for the *New York World*. Readers were appalled by what they read and demanded that changes be made at asylums. The readers were also impressed by Bly's bravery. Many people bought the newspaper to follow her columns.

Because of her daring work on Blackwell's Island, the *New York World* hired her as a full-time journalist. She later wrote a book about her experiences, titled, *Ten Days in a Mad-House.*[6]

Nellie's book shed light on the ill treatment that people received in asylums.

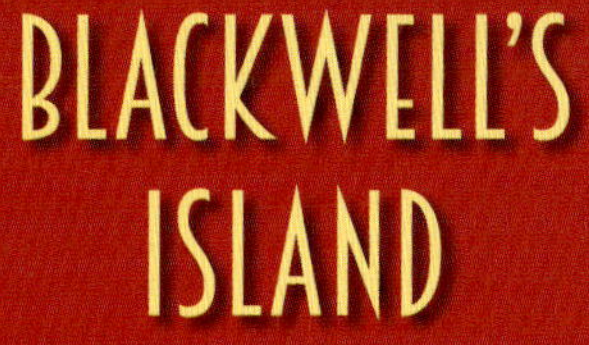

BLACKWELL'S ISLAND

New York City is made up of several islands. The long, skinny island of Manhattan is in between the Hudson River on the west and the East River on the east. Long Island lies between the East River and the Atlantic Ocean. The Bronx is north of Manhattan, across a stretch of river called the Spuyten Duyvel ("Spitting Devil"), which is not an island.

In the middle of the East River is another long and skinny island, but it is much smaller than Manhattan. It is called Roosevelt Island now, but in Nellie Bly's time, it was called Blackwell's Island.

In the 1800s, Blackwell's Island was home to a prison, an insane asylum, and later a hospital. No one lived on the isolated island unless they were patients or inmates. When Bly went undercover for the first time, she posed as a patient at Blackwell's asylum for women.

By 1968, the old buildings were no longer in use. They were demolished and replaced by high-rise apartment buildings. The island's name was changed in 1973 to honor Franklin D. Roosevelt. Today, about 12,000 people live on Roosevelt Island. It is connected to the rest of the city by a subway stop, a tram, and a bridge. Residents say it is quiet on Roosevelt Island, and their homes have panoramic views of the city.

After Nellie published her articles on Blackwell's Island, she went on to write similar investigative pieces. To get the real scoop for her stories, she posed as different kinds of people. For one story, she got herself arrested so that she could expose the unfair treatment of women in jails.[1] To get the inside information for another story, she applied for work at a factory in New York. In this article, she revealed what it was like to work from sunup to sundown in appalling conditions for very little pay.[2]

For another story, she moved into a tenement apartment in New York's Lower East Side. This was an extremely crowded part of the city where many new immigrants squeezed into tiny apartments. On one block, some 3,530 people lived. "No other block upon this earth, or same space of ground, is so densely populated. Thirty-five hundred and thirty-two people would make a good-sized town,

Nellie Bly was a distinguished, fashionable lady of her time period. She was also one of the most famous reporters in the city.

Laundry dries behind tenement housing in the year 1900. Tenements in New York were often filthy and crowded. Millions of people lived in New York's tenements in the late 1800s.

and towns of smaller population have a mayor, a postmaster, constables, churches and bankers all of their own," Nellie Bly explained.[3] During the hottest part of the summer, she lived in an apartment on this block. The tenement building was hot, dark, filthy, and brimming with people. After living there for just a few days, Nellie was able to gather enough information to reveal just how bad the conditions were in that part of the city.

Nellie's stories made her a pioneer in journalism. She was one of the first journalists to do undercover investigative reporting. Her stories were enormously popular. Many readers looked forward to what "stunt" she would pull in her next piece. But her stories also shed light on the many problems in society and made people believe that change was necessary. Her stories also inspired other journalists to become "stunt reporters," too.

In 1889, Nellie came up with her biggest idea yet. She read about Phileas Fogg, the main character from Jules Verne's book *Around the World in 80 Days*. She thought that if this make-believe character could circumnavigate the world, so could she. But she wouldn't do it in 80 days. She would do it in less than that!

To go on her trip, she had to first convince her editors at the *New York World*. She needed them to agree so that they would pay for her to cover the story. At first they said no. They didn't think that a woman should travel alone on such a possibly dangerous journey. But Nellie told them if they

Phileas Fogg used many modes of transportation, just as Nellie Bly did.

Bly's newspaper, the *New York World*, announced "She's Broken Every Record!" when she returned.

chose to send a man instead, she would just get another newspaper to send her. They didn't want to lose her. She was one of their top writers. Finally they agreed to send her on the trip.[4]

When Nellie returned from her grand adventure around the world, she continued her reporting as an undercover journalist. One of her most famous stories during the 1890s was on the Pullman Strike in 1894.

During this strike, the railroad workers were protesting unfair treatment. Their pay had just been slashed, but the prices for housing and food in the company-owned town remained high. The families were near starvation. The workers went on strike to demand an increase in wages, better working conditions, and better living conditions.

The railroad in the late 1800s was extremely important to the United States. Many people and companies used the railroad to travel and ship goods across the country. Without railroad workers, the railroad couldn't run.

Many people were upset at the railroad workers, thinking that they were just being greedy. Nellie Bly thought this a little too—at first. But then she went undercover to find out the truth. She discovered that the workers were forced to live in the Pullman houses in order to work at the railroad. The rent was much higher

The Illinois National Guard stands between strikers and the Arcade Building in Pullman, a neighborhood in Chicago, in 1894.

than what they would pay elsewhere. One man told her, "I was also reduced from $3 a day to $1.50. My rent was $9.50, and at one pay day I had only been given 13 days' work. After they took out my rent I had a check for one cent to live on for two weeks and keep my wife and child."[5]

In her article for the *New York World* on July 11, 1894, Nellie wrote, "I thought the inhabitants of the model town of Pullman hadn't a reason on earth to complain. With this belief I visited the town, intending in my articles to denounce the rioters as bloodthirsty strikers. Before I had been half a day in Pullman, I was the most bitter striker in the town."[6]

Nellie Bly didn't keep quiet about injustice. She was known as a champion of the people.

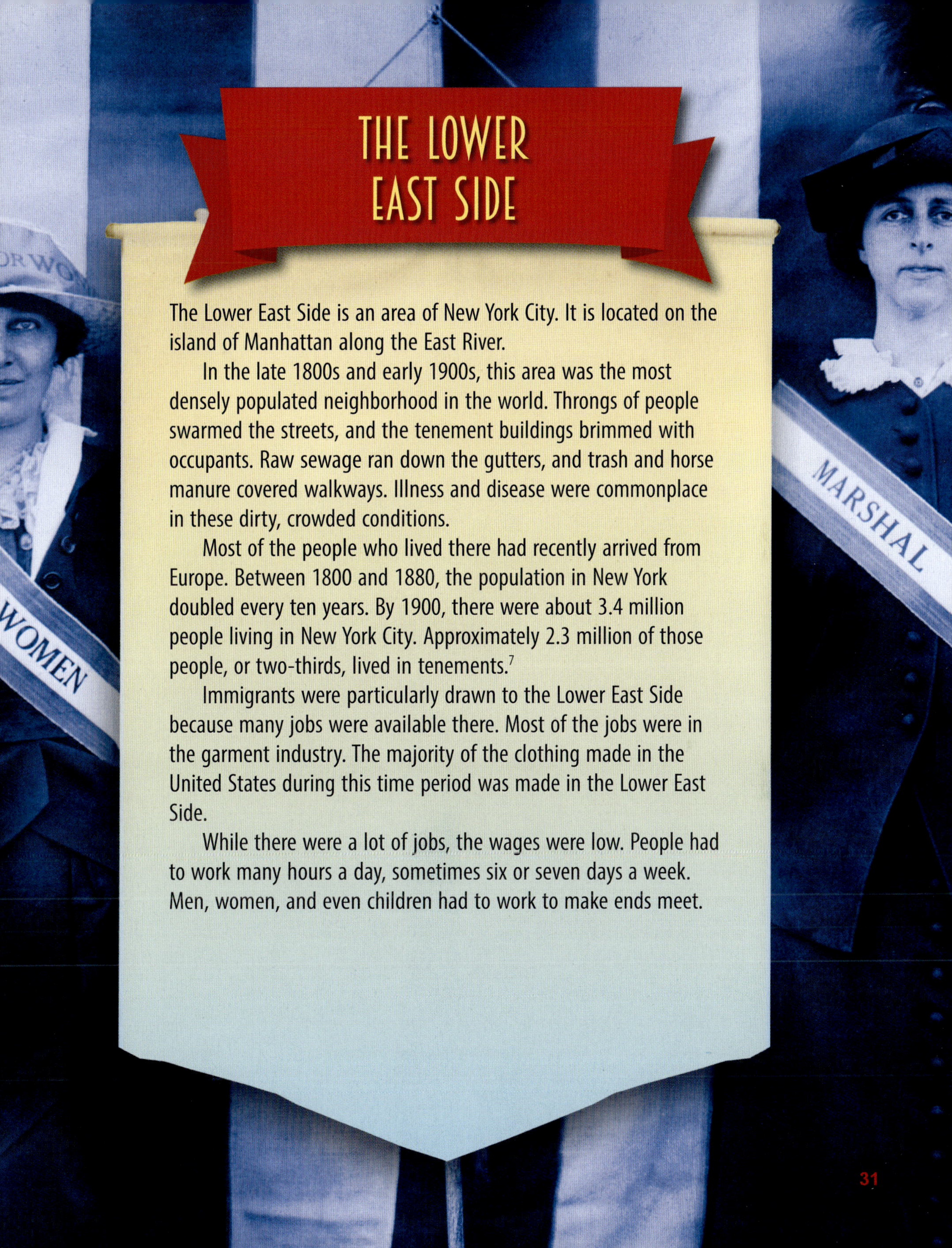

THE LOWER EAST SIDE

The Lower East Side is an area of New York City. It is located on the island of Manhattan along the East River.

In the late 1800s and early 1900s, this area was the most densely populated neighborhood in the world. Throngs of people swarmed the streets, and the tenement buildings brimmed with occupants. Raw sewage ran down the gutters, and trash and horse manure covered walkways. Illness and disease were commonplace in these dirty, crowded conditions.

Most of the people who lived there had recently arrived from Europe. Between 1800 and 1880, the population in New York doubled every ten years. By 1900, there were about 3.4 million people living in New York City. Approximately 2.3 million of those people, or two-thirds, lived in tenements.[7]

Immigrants were particularly drawn to the Lower East Side because many jobs were available there. Most of the jobs were in the garment industry. The majority of the clothing made in the United States during this time period was made in the Lower East Side.

While there were a lot of jobs, the wages were low. People had to work many hours a day, sometimes six or seven days a week. Men, women, and even children had to work to make ends meet.

In 1895, Nellie met a millionaire industrialist and manufacturer from Brooklyn, New York. His name was Robert Livingston Seaman. After just two weeks, she and Robert were married. Many people were stunned at the quick engagement and marriage. They were also shocked that she would marry someone so much older. Robert was 73 years old and Nellie was only 31.[1]

Nellie and Robert were married for nearly 10 years. They lived at 15 West Thirty-Seventh Street in Manhattan.[2] During the late 1800s, this was a prominent area for wealthy New Yorkers. Today, high-rise hotels and office buildings sit on this spot on Fashion Avenue.

During her marriage, Nellie stopped working as a journalist and instead focused on learning all about Robert's companies. He was the president of the American Steel Barrel Company and the

Nellie married a man much older than she. The two had a happy ten-year marriage before he passed away in 1904.

Oil continues to be shipped all over the world in 55-gallon drums. They were invented at Iron Clad.

Iron Clad Manufacturing Company. It was smart that Nellie spent time learning about these companies. When Robert died in 1904, she was the one in charge.[3]

Nellie had many big goals for the companies. She wanted to improve production. Under her leadership, the company began manufacturing the world's first practical 55-gallon oil drum. This leak-proof container allowed oil to be shipped without any spills.[4]

Nellie also wanted to improve the conditions for her workers. First, she increased their wages. Second, she provided facilities for them to use. She built recreation centers that offered fitness programs. She built libraries and offered classes so the employees could learn how to read.[5]

Nellie successfully ran the companies for about ten years. She was the only woman in the world at that time to run such large industries. Yet, she didn't find out until it was too late that some of her employees were dishonest. They had been stealing money from the company. She eventually lost nearly everything when the companies went bankrupt.[6]

In 1914, Nellie left New York City for Vienna, Austria. She was trying to find people who would loan her money to pay off her business debts.[7] World War I started shortly after she arrived in Austria. She unfortunately couldn't find anyone to pay her debts, but she started writing articles about the events of the Great War unfolding in front of her.

Nellie went right to work in Vienna researching and writing stories for the papers in New York. She had missed the world of journalism. She had written only a few articles since she had married. Now, she was America's first female war correspondent.

During the early days of World War I, Nellie visited the front lines often. She climbed into the trenches to see what life was like for the soldiers.[8] Her articles allowed Americans to really understand what was going on in the war. She didn't work just as a

Nellie interviews an Austrian army officer in 1914.

journalist during her time in Austria. She also worked to help Austrian families whose husbands and fathers had died in the war.[9]

In 1919, the war ended. After living for nearly five years in Europe, Nellie returned to New York. She didn't have much money left from her husband's companies, so she rented a room at the Hotel McAlpin.[10] Located in Manhattan's Herald Square, this hotel is near the Macy's department store where the city's Thanksgiving Day Parade starts every year.

Since her husband's fortune was gone, Nellie had no choice but to go back to work. She didn't mind, though, since she thoroughly enjoyed her job as a journalist. *The New York Evening Journal* hired Nellie as one of their journalists. They gave her a regular column in the paper. In this column, she would respond to letters written by readers. She gave advice to people who needed help with problems or concerns in their lives.[11]

Often the people who wrote in to her column needed more than just

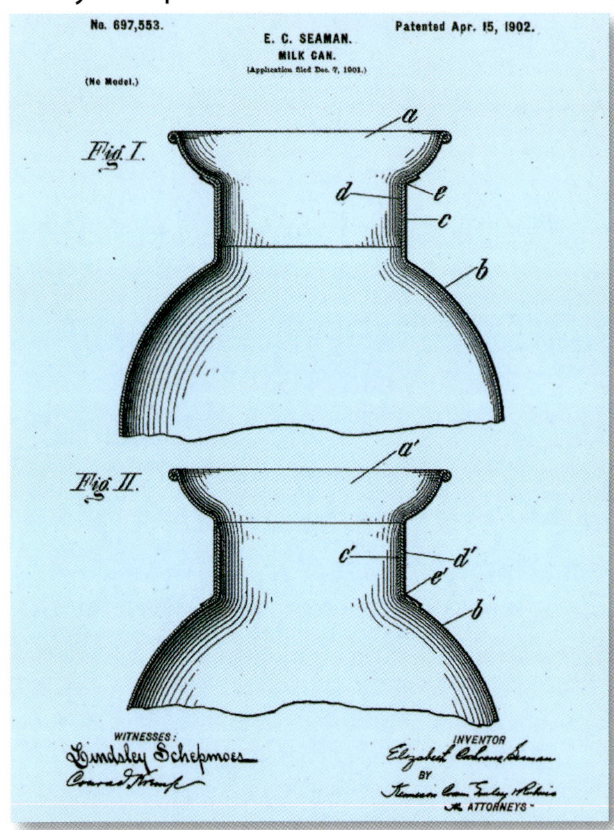

Nellie came up with her own ideas, too. This is a patent for a milk can cap that she invented.

advice. They needed real help. She would personally try to do what she could to help them.

Nellie always had a spot in her heart for people who were suffering. That's why she had focused so much of her career on writing about real problems in society. At this time of her life, she began helping orphans in New York. She had spent time doing that in Vienna and figured she could help the children of her country, too. She took in orphan children who needed a place to stay and helped find families to adopt them.[12]

Nellie Bly became ill in January of 1922. By the end of the month, she had been rushed to St. Mark's Hospital in Manhattan. She passed away of pneumonia on January 27. She was only 57 years old.

Newspapers around the world announced her death. But perhaps the most significant tribute came from Arthur Brisbane. He was her friend and editor at *The New York Evening Journal*.

Nellie will always be remembered for her adventurous spirit and her willingness to "get the story."

Nellie was a fashionable woman, even in her later years.

He said, "Nellie Bly was THE BEST REPORTER IN AMERICA and that is saying a good deal. . . . She takes with her from this earth all that she cared for, an honorable name, the respect and affection of her fellow workers, the memory of good fights well fought, and of the many good deeds never to be forgotten by those who had no friend but Nellie Bly. Happy the man or woman that can leave as good a record."[13]

Nellie's books are still available online and in libraries today.

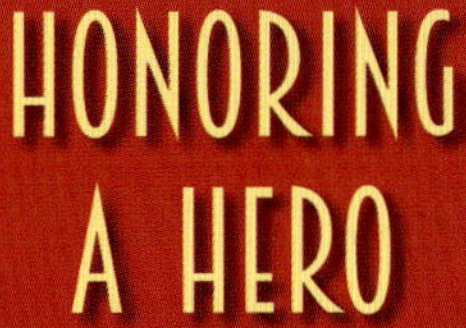

Nellie Bly was buried in Woodlawn Cemetery, one of the largest cemeteries in New York. Located north of Manhattan in the Bronx, it is a national historic landmark.

When she was buried, her estate didn't have the money to pay for a headstone. Her grave was bare for more than fifty years.

In 1978, the New York Press Club wanted to right that wrong. They pooled their money and paid for a headstone. It is inscribed with the words:

Dedicated June 22, 1978
To
Nellie Bly
Elizabeth Cochrane Seaman
By the New York Press Club
In Honor of
A Famous News Reporter
May 5, 1864 – Jan 27, 1922

Nellie Bly

39

1864   Elizabeth Jane Cochran is born on May 5, 1864, in Cochrans Mills, Pennsylvania. She will later be known as Nellie Bly.

1870   Elizabeth's father dies, leaving his family penniless.

1872   Jules Verne publishes *Around the World in 80 Days.*

1879   Elizabeth enrolls at the State Normal School in Indiana, Pennsylvania, but has to drop out after one semester.

1885   She begins writing for *The Pittsburgh Dispatch*, using the pen name of Nellie Bly. She soon quits *The Pittsburgh Dispatch* and begins working as a freelance journalist. She writes articles from Mexico and sells them to the *Dispatch*.

1887   She moves to New York City and writes about conditions in a mental hospital for women. She continues writing investigative stories for the *New York World*.

1889   On November 14, Nellie Bly begins her round-the-world journey.

1890   She completes her circumnavigation on January 25.

1894   She investigates conditions of Pullman workers who are striking for better wages.

1895   Bly marries Robert Livingston Seaman. She begins learning about his businesses, the American Steel Barrel Company and the Iron Clad Manufacturing Company.

1904   Robert dies, and Nellie leads the companies. She works to improve conditions for the workers there.

1914   After losing the companies to some dishonest employees, Bly moves to Vienna, Austria. While there, World War I is declared. Bly becomes the first American female war correspondent.

1919 She returns to New York and begins writing a regular advice column for *The New York Evening Journal*. She also regularly helps New York orphans find homes.

1922 In January, Bly dies of pneumonia. She is buried in New York's Woodlawn Cemetery.

Nellie Bly

Chapter 1

1. Nellie Bly. *Around the World in 72 Days*. New York; The Pictorial Weeklies Company, 1890. Available at https://digital.library.upenn.edu/women/bly/world/world.html

2. Roma Panganiban. "Nellie Bly's 72 Day Trip Around the World." *Mental Floss*. September 17, 2013. Available at https://www.mentalfloss.com/article/52745/nellie-blys-72-day-trip-around-world

3. Bly.

4. Brian Phillips. "72 Days, Six Hours, and 11 Minutes: How a Pioneering Journalist Won a Race Around the World in 1889." *Grantland*. November 14, 2014. Available at https://grantland.com/the-triangle/nellie-bly-around-the-world-in-seventy-two-days/

5. Bly.

6. Ibid.

7. Ibid.

8. Ibid.

9. "Focus: Nellie Bly." *Orange County Register*. November 13, 2014. Available at https://www.ocregister.com/2014/11/13/focus-nellie-bly/

Chapter 2

1. "Nellie Bly tells of her arrest as a British Spy," *Los Angeles Herald*. January 12, 1915. Available at https://cdnc.ucre.edu/cgi-bin/cdnc?a=d&d=LAH19150112.2.23&e=-------en--20--1--txt-txIN--------

2. Phil Edwards. "How Nellie Bly Became a Victorian Sensation and Changed Journalism Forever." *Vox*. May 5, 2015. Available at https://www.vox.com/2015/5/5/8548361/nellie-bly-journalist

3. Arlisha R. Norwood, updated by Marian Brandman. "Nellie Bly." National Women's History Museum. Available at https://www.womenshistory.org/education-resources/biographies/nellie-bly-0

4. Hannah Keyser. "The Story That Launched Nellie Bly's Famed Journalism Career." *Mental Floss*. May 5, 2015. Available at https://www.mentalfloss.com/article/63759/story-launched-nellie-blys-famed-journalism-career

5. Miranda Spencer. "No One Said No to Nellie." *Biography*. April 1998.

6. Alice Gregory. "Nellie Bly's Lessons in Writing What You Want To." *New Yorker*. May 14, 2014. Available at https://www.newyorker.com/books/page-turner/nellie-blys-lessons-in-writing-what-you-want-to

Chapter 3

1. Amber Paranick. "'Behind Asylum Bars:' Nellie Bly Reporting from Blackwell's Island." *Library of Congress Blogs*. November 8, 2022. Available at https://blogs.loc.gov/headlinesandheroes/2022/11/nellie-bly-blackwells-island

2. Miranda Spencer. "No One Said No to Nellie." *Biography*. April 1998.

3. Nellie Bly. *Ten Days in a Mad-House*. New York: Norman L. Munro, 1887. Available at https://digital.library.upenn.edu/women/bly/madhouse/madhouse.html

4. "In an Insane Hospital." *The Anderson Intelligencer*. October 20, 1887.

5. Bly.

6. Ibid.

Chapter 4

1. Nellie Bly. "Nellie Bly a Prisoner." *New York World*. February 24, 1889. Available at https://thegrandarchive.wordpress.com/nellie-bly-a-prisoner/

2. Nellie Bly. "The Girls Who Make Boxes." *New York World*. November 27, 1887. Available at https://thegrandarchive.wordpress.com/the-girls-who-make-boxes/

3. Nellie Bly. "In the Biggest New York Tenement." *New York World*. August 5, 1894. Available at https://thegrandarchive.wordpress.com/in-the-biggest-new-york-tenement/

4. Brian Phillips. "72 Days, Six Hours, and 11 Minutes: How a Pioneering Journalist Won a Race Around the World in 1889." *Grantland*. November 14, 2014. Available at https://grantland.com/the-triangle/nellie-bly-around-the-world-in-seventy-two-days/

5. "Nellie Bly on the Pullman Strike." *Los Angeles Herald*. July 24, 1894. Available at https://cdnc.ucr.edu/?a=d&d=LAH18940724.2.30&e=-------en--20--1--txt-txIN--------

6. Nellie Bly. "Nellie Bly in Pullman." *New York World*. July 11, 1894.

7. "Tenements." History.com. Available at https://www.history.com/topics/immigration/tenements

Chapter 5

1. Jone Johnson Lewis. "Biography of Nellie Bly, Investigative Journalist, World Traveler." *ThoughtCo*. Updated March 10, 2019. Available at https://www.thoughtco.com/nellie-bly-biography-3528562

2. "Nellie Bly, Journalist, Dies of Pneumonia," *The New York Times*. January 28, 1922. Available at https://archive.nytimes.com/www.nytimes.com/learning/general/onthisday/bday/0505.html

3. "Remarkable Nellie Bly's Oil Drum." American Oil and Gas Historical Society. Available at https://aoghs.org/transportation/nellie-bly-oil-drum/#google_vignette

4. Ibid.

5. Lewis.

6. Ibid.

7. "Remarkable Nellie Bly's Oil Drum."

8. Lewis.

9. Gena Philibert-Ortega. "Remembering Intrepid Nellie Bly, World War I Reporter." *Genealogy Bank*. May 18, 2017. Available at https://blog.genealogybank.com/remembering-intrepid-nellie-bly-world-war-i-reporter.html

10. "Nellie Bly, Journalist, Dies of Pneumonia."

11. Philibert-Ortega.

12. Lewis.

13. Amanda Matthews. "*The Girl Puzzle* Concept: Nellie Bly and the Women and Girls for whom she Advocated: Stories Behind the Faces." *The Girl Puzzle*. 2024. Available at https://www.thegirlpuzzle.com/concept

Works Consulted

Barcousky, Len. "Eyewitness 1890: Pittsburgh Welcomes Home Globe-Trotting Nellie Bly." *Pittsburgh Post-Gazette.* August 22, 2009. https://www.post-gazette.com/community-eyewitness/2009/08/23/Eyewitness-1890-Pittsburgh-welcomes-home-globe-trotting-Nellie-Bly/stories/200908230164

Bly, Nellie. *10 Days in a Mad-House.* https://digital.library.upenn.edu/women/bly/madhouse/madhouse.html

Bly, Nellie. *Around the World in 72 Days.* New York: The Pictorial Weeklies Company, 1890. https://digital.library.upenn.edu/women/bly/world/world.html

Bly, Nellie. *The Complete Works of Nellie Bly.* CreateSpace Independent Publishing Platform, 2015.

Bly, Nellie. "The Girls Who Make Boxes." *New York World.* November 27. 1887. https://thegrandarchive.wordpress.com/the-girls-who-make-boxes/

Bly, Nellie. "In the Biggest New York Tenement." *New York World.* August 5, 1894. https://thegrandarchive.wordpress.com/in-the-biggest-new-york-tenement/

Bly, Nellie. "Nellie Bly a Prisoner." *New York World.* February 24, 1889. https://thegrandarchive.wordpress.com/nellie-bly-a-prisoner/

Bly, Nellie. "Nellie Bly in Pullman." *New York World.* July 11, 1894.

Edwards, Phil. "How Nellie Bly Became a Victorian Sensation and Changed Journalism Forever." *Vox.* May 5, 2015. https://www.vox.com/2015/5/5/8548361/nellie-bly-journalist

"Focus: Nellie Bly." *Orange County Register.* November 13, 2014. https://www.ocregister.com/2014/11/13/focus-nellie-bly/

Gregory, Alice. "Nellie Bly's Lessons in Writing What You Want To." *New Yorker.* May 14, 2014. https://www.newyorker.com/books/page-turner/nellie-blys-lessons-in-writing-what-you-want-to

Keyser, Hannah. "The Story That Launched Nellie Bly's Famed Journalism Career." *Mental Floss*. May 5, 2015. https://mentalfloss.com/article/63759/story-launched-nellie-blys-famed-journalism-career

Lewis, Jone Johnson. "Nellie Bly: Investigative Journalist and Around-the-World Traveler." *ThoughtCo*. June 2, 2017. https://www.thoughtco.com/nellie-bly-biography-3528562

"Nellie Bly, Journalist, Dies of Pneumonia." *The New York Times*. January 28, 1922. https://archive.nytimes.com/www.nytimes.com/learning/general/onthisday/bday/0505.html

"Nellie Bly on the Pullman Strike." *Los Angeles Herald*. July 24, 1894. https://cdnc.ucr.edu/cgi-bin/cdnc?a=d&d=LAH18940724.2.30&e=-------en--20--1--txt-txIN--------

"Nellie Bly Tells of Her Arrest as a British Spy." *Los Angeles Herald*. January 12, 1915. https://cdnc.ucr.edu/cgi-bin/cdnc?a=d&d=LAH19150112.2.23&e=-------en--20--1--txt-txIN--------

Norwood, Arlisha R. "Nellie Bly." National Women's History Museum. https://www.womenshistory.org/education-resources/biographies/nellie-bly-0

Panganiban, Roma. "Nellie Bly's 72 Day Trip Around the World." *Mental Floss*. September 17, 2013. https://mentalfloss.com/article/52745/nellie-blys-72-day-trip-around-world

Philibert-Ortega, Gena. "Remembering Intrepid Nellie Bly, World War I Reporter." *Genealogy Bank*. May 18, 2017. https://blog.genealogybank.com/remembering-intrepid-nellie-bly-world-war-i-reporter.html

Phillips, Brian. "72 Days, Six Hours, and 11 Minutes: How a Pioneering Journalist Won a Race Around the World in 1889," *Grantland*. November 14, 2014. https://grantland.com/the-triangle/nellie-bly-around-the-world-in-seventy-two-days/

"Remarkable Nellie Bly's Oil Drum." American Oil and Gas Historical Society. https://aoghs.org/transportation/nellie-bly-oil-drum/

Spencer, Miranda. "No One Said No to Nellie." *Biography*. April 1998. Vol. 2 Issue 4. pp. 60–66.

"Tenements." History.com. https://www.history.com/topics/tenements

Books

Christensen, Bonnie. *The Daring Nellie: America's Star Reporter*. New York: Knopf Books for Young Readers, 2013.

Goodman, Matthew. *Eighty Days: Nellie Bly and Elizabeth Bisland's History-Making Race Around the World*. New York: Ballantine Books, 2014.

Mahoney, Ellen. *Nellie Bly and Investigative Journalism for Kids: Mighty Muckrakers from the Golden Age to Today, with 21 Activities*. Chicago: Chicago Review Press, 2015.

Noyes, Deborah. *Ten Days a Madwoman: The Daring Life and Turbulent Times of the Original "Girl" Reporter, Nellie Bly*. New York: Puffin Books, 2017.

On the Internet

Articles by Nellie Bly
https://www.historicjournalism.com/nellie-bly.html
Nellie Bly Online
https://nellieblyonline.net/
Travel Channel Video on Nellie Bly
https://www.travelchannel.com/videos/nellie-blys-undercover-story-0211918

bankrupt (BANK-rupt)—Unable to pay debts.

boardinghouse (BOR-ding-house)—A house in which different people rent the bedrooms and share the other rooms.

circumnavigate (sir-kum-NAV-ih-gayt)—To go all the way around something, such as the earth.

column (KAH-lum)—A regular feature in a newspaper.

committed (kuh-MIH-tid)—Ordered to go to a hospital for a long stay.

correspondent (kor-eh-SPON-dent)—A person who writes letters or articles for a newspaper on a regular basis.

inheritance (in-HAYR-ih-tints)—Money or property passed down through a family.

insane asylum (in-SAYN uh-SY-lum)—A place where mentally ill people are hospitalized. Today, this type of hospital is called a mental institution or hospital for the mentally ill.

journalist (JUR-nuh-list)—A writer for a newspaper or magazine.

manufacturing (man-yoo-FAK-chur-ing)—The business of making goods using machinery.

minstrel (MIN-strul)—A show that features short performances of music, dance, and comedy.

pen name—A fake name used by writers to hide their identity.

platform—A place where passengers get on and off a train.

pneumonia (noo-MOH-nyuh)—A dangerous illness of the lungs.

poverty (PAH-ver-tee)—The condition of being extremely poor.

rickshaw (RIK-shaw)—A light vehicle with two wheels that is pulled by one or two people.

sampan (SAM-pan)—A traditional Chinese flat-bottomed boat.

semester (seh-MES-ter)—Half a school year.

souvenir (soo-vih-NEER)—An item you buy or collect on travels in order to remember them.

strike—A time when workers refuse to work in order to get their employers to treat them better.

tenement (TEH-nuh-ment)—A building or block of overcrowded and poorly maintained apartments in poor neighborhoods.

undercover (UN-der-KUH-ver)—Involved in some kind of secret work, often taking on a different name or identity.

will—An official legal document that details what you would like to happen with your property after you die.

American Steel Barrel Company   32

Around the World in 80 Days   4, 5, 11, 27

Associated Press   17

Augusta Victoria   4

Bellevue Hospital   21

Blackwell's Island   21, 22, 23

Bly, Nellie

    around-the-world trip   4, 5, 6–10, 11, 13, 27–28, 38

    in asylum for women   19, 20–22, 23, 24

    in Austria   35–36

    birth of   12

    childhood   12, 14–15

    death of   37–38, 39

    education of   14–15

    fashion   13, 25

    as industrialist   32, 34–35, 36

    as journalist   8, 9, 15–16, 17, 18, 20-22, 24, 25, 26–30, 35–37, 39

    marriage of   32, 33, 34

    in Mexico   16, 17

    in New York City   8, 9, 11, 18, 20, 22, 23, 24, 26, 31, 35, 36, 37, 39

    and orphans   37

    pen name   12

    in Pittsburgh, Pennsylvania   10, 15, 17, 18

    and Pullman Strike   28–30

    in tenements   24, 26, 31

Brisbane, Arthur   37, 38

Brown, Nellie   20

Cochran, Elizabeth Jane   (*see* Bly, Nellie)

Cochran's Mills, Pennsylvania   12

Cockerill, John   18

Fogg, Phileas   4, 5, 6, 9, 10, 11, 27

Foster, J. Heron   17

Herald Square   36

Iron Clad Manufacturing Company   34

Lower East Side (Manhattan)   24, 31

Mental illness   19, 20–22, 23

New York Evening Journal, The   36, 37

New York Press Club   39

New York World   18, 20, 22, 27, 28, 30

Oceanic   9

Pittsburgh Dispatch, The   15, 17, 18

Port Said, Egypt   6

psychiatry   19

Pulitzer, Joseph   18

Pullman Strike   28–30

Roosevelt, Franklin D.   23

Roosevelt Island   23

sampan   8

Seaman, Robert Livingston (husband)   32

Six Months in Mexico   16

State Normal School   14

telegrams   8

Ten Days in a Mad-House   22

tenements   24, 26, 31

Verne, Jules   4, 5, 11, 27

women's rights   15, 17

World War I   35–36